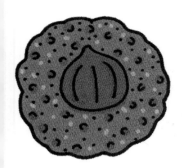
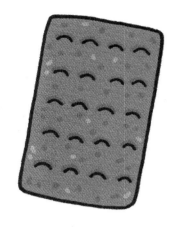

Chocolate Box

10 MUSICAL TREATS FOR FLUTE AND PIANO

PAUL HARRIS

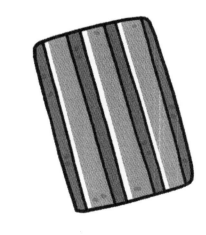

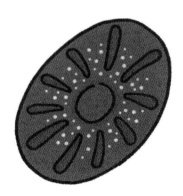

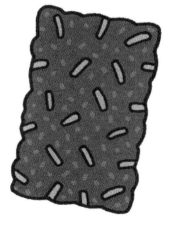

Novello Publishing Limited
14-15 Berners Street, London W1T 3LJ

Exclusive Distributors:
Hal Leonard
7777 West Bluemound Road, Milwaukee, WI 53213
Email: info@halleonard.com

Hal Leonard Europe Limited
42 Wigmore Street, Marylebone, London WIU 2 RY
Email: info@halleonardeurope.com

Hal Leonard Australia Pty. Ltd.
4 Lentara Court, Cheltenham, Victoria 9132, Australia
Email: info@halleonard.com.au

This book © Copyright 2002 Novello Publishing Limited.
Order No. NOV016203
ISBN 0-7119-9644-X

Music Processed by Andrew Shiels.
Cover design by Chloë Alexander.
Illustration by Jo Moore.
Printed in EU.

www.halleonard.com

CONTENTS

1 Hazelnote Crunch

2 Minty Minuet

poco rit.　　　　A tempo

9

3 Dark Chocolate Truffle Trot

4 Toffee Tango

15

5 Strawberry Sarabande

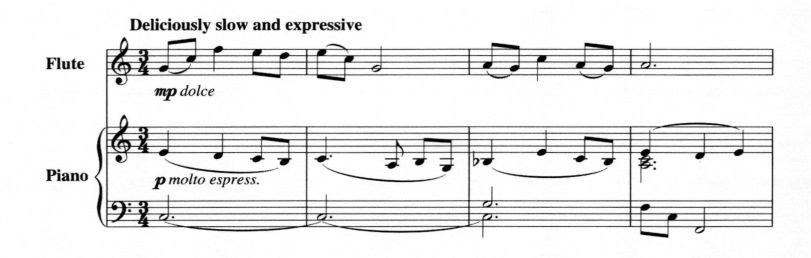

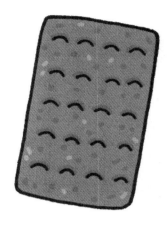

Chocolate Box

10
MUSICAL
TREATS
FOR FLUTE
AND PIANO

PAUL HARRIS

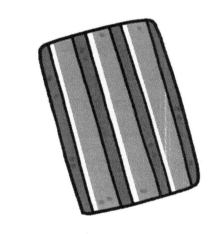

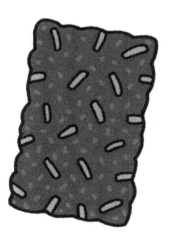
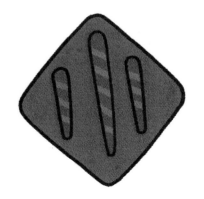

Novello Publishing Limited
14-15 Berners Street, London W1T 3LJ

CONTENTS

1 Hazelnote Crunch

2 Minty Minuet

3 Dark Chocolate Truffle Trot

4 Toffee Tango

5 Strawberry Sarabande

Deliciously slow and expressive

mp dolce

mf

poco rall.   A tempo

mp

cresc.

poco rall.

mf

6 Viennese Vanilla Valse

7 Mocha Baroqua

Handel with care

8 Caramel Carousel

9 Fudge Fandango

With a Spanish flavour

10 Maple Nut Rag

6 Viennese Vanilla Valse

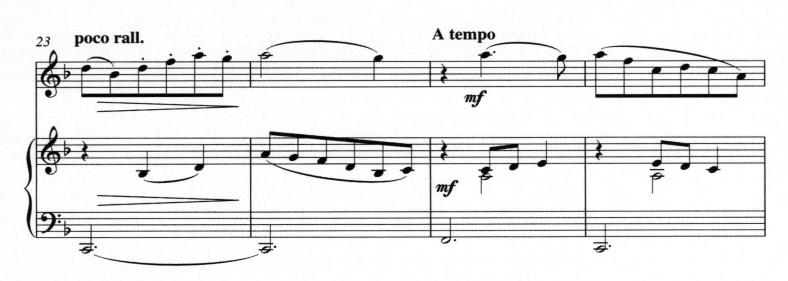

21

7 Mocha Baroqua

Handel with care

8 Caramel Carousel

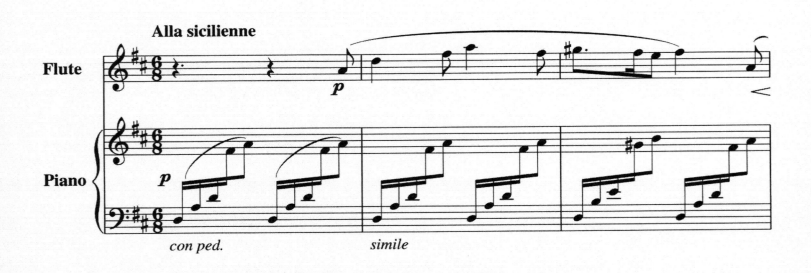

9 Fudge Fandango

With a Spanish flavour

29

10 Maple Nut Rag